FINANCIAL LITERACY

MANAGING DEBT

By Alexis Burling

CONTENT CONSULTANT
Robert Kelchen, Assistant Professor
Department of Education Leadership,
Management and Policy
Seton Hall University

Essential Library

An Imprint of Abdo Publishing | abdobooks.com

ABDOBOOKS.COM

Published by Abdo Publishing, a division of ABDO, PO Box 398166, Minneapolis, Minnesota 55439. Copyright © 2020 by Abdo Consulting Group, Inc. International copyrights reserved in all countries. No part of this book may be reproduced in any form without written permission from the publisher. Essential Library™ is a trademark and logo of Abdo Publishing.

Printed in the United States of America, North Mankato, Minnesota.
032019
092019

THIS BOOK CONTAINS
RECYCLED MATERIALS

Cover Photo: Joy Seulay/Shutterstock Images
Interior Photos: Shutterstock Images, 5, 18, 21, 41, 68, 72, 97; Red Line Editorial, 6, 17, 48, 67; Jason Cox/Shutterstock Images, 8; Gregor Bister/iStockphoto, 15; Monkey Business Images/iStockphoto, 27; Dragon Images/Shutterstock Images, 28; Wave Break Media/iStockphoto, 31, 75; Ian Allenden/Alamy, 34; Panumas Yanuthai/Shutterstock Images, 39; iStockphoto, 44, 55, 61, 62, 65, 76, 81, 91; Davizro Photography/Shutterstock Images, 53; Mango Star Studio/iStockphoto, 87; Rawpixel/iStockphoto, 94

Editor: Alyssa Krekelberg
Series Designer: Colleen McLaren

LIBRARY OF CONGRESS CONTROL NUMBER: 2018966055

PUBLISHER'S CATALOGING-IN-PUBLICATION DATA

Names: Burling, Alexis, author.
Title: Managing debt / by Alexis Burling.
Description: Minneapolis, Minnesota : Abdo Publishing, 2020 | Series: Financial literacy | Includes online resources and index.
Identifiers: ISBN 9781532119149 (lib. bdg.) | ISBN 9781532173325 (ebook)
Subjects: LCSH: Debt--Juvenile literature. | Debt relief--Juvenile literature. | Cost of debt--Juvenile literature. | Debt collection laws--Juvenile literature.
Classification: DDC 332.024--dc23

TNF
MONEY
11/12/19

So all readers may use the worksheets, please complete the exercises in your own notebook.

CONTENTS

CHAPTER ONE

SWIMMING IN DEBT

It was one month before her eighteenth birthday and Jasmine was thrilled. After months of deliberation, she had finally figured out how she wanted to celebrate and was almost finished with the planning process. All of her closest friends were invited. She asked some of her older brother Ari's friends to come to the later events, too. The more, the merrier.

First, Jasmine and her best friend, Erika, were going out to dinner at a new sushi place in town. It was a little expensive, but Jasmine felt that it was worth it. Then, they'd meet up with a few other girls and go dancing. At the end of the night, everyone else would meet at the beach for a bonfire. She'd already bought plenty of refreshments and hired a DJ. If all went as she hoped, Jasmine's beach party bonanza would be the talk of the school.

Jasmine made a list of all the things she had already done for the party to see what she had left to

To help avoid debt, people should be aware of how much money they spend.

TEEN SPENDING[1]

According to a 2015 study, teens spend most of their money on food. They also shell out money for clothing, cars, accessories and cosmetics, shoes, video games, and electronics.

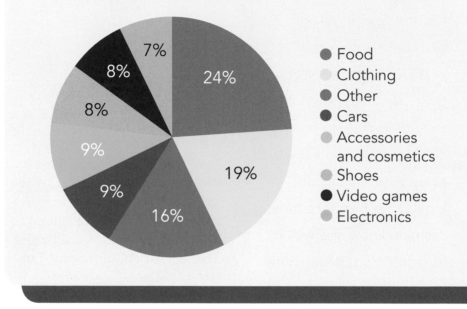

- Food
- Clothing
- Other
- Cars
- Accessories and cosmetics
- Shoes
- Video games
- Electronics

do. She also wrote down how much she had already charged on her starter credit card and how much she might expect to pay for the remaining expenses. Her new outfit had cost $175—at the last minute, she had thrown in some new makeup and shoes. The decorations and snacks for the beach party totaled $265. The DJ she booked was expensive at $650. But when she asked around at school, everyone said this guy was the best. The bill for the sushi dinner would probably be at least $65, including appetizers, soda, and a tip. Beverages and snacks at the dancing club would clock in at around $25.

More than $1,000 seemed like a lot of money to spend on one day. But Jasmine knew she could handle it. At least she thought she could, until she showed her credit card bill to her mom—a bill she couldn't even come close to paying off right away. After taking one look at her mother's face, Jasmine knew she was in for a letdown. It was time for the finance talk.

REALITY CHECK

What Jasmine's mother knew, and what her daughter hadn't considered, was that Jasmine was forming unhealthy spending

LEARNING ABOUT MONEY

Jasmine and her mom have a close relationship. Though they don't agree on everything, they feel comfortable enough with each other to have honest discussions about money. But not all teenagers are close with their parent or guardian. In fact, many parental figures have financial troubles of their own. Still, it's important for young people to find someone they trust who can explain what debt is. If a relative isn't available, teens can ask a family friend, teacher, or librarian for guidance. A representative at a local bank might also be able to help.

Credit card charges can add up fast if people aren't aware of their spending habits.

habits. Yes, Jasmine had a part-time job as a barista at a coffee shop and her income would help her pay for some of the party's cost. Jasmine's mom planned to contribute too, even though she was a single mom working two jobs. But she wasn't pleased that Jasmine had already put more than $1,000 on her new credit card.

Plus, Jasmine already owed her brother more than $1,000. He had loaned her cash for a down payment

TAKING CONTROL OF MONEY

According to a 2017 study, one in five teens in the United States lacks basic financial literacy skills.[2] But finance expert Suze Orman says learning how to balance a budget and knowing the value of earning a paycheck is critical to becoming a responsible adult.

"Instilling the power of earning money is one of the greatest lessons—and gifts—a parent can give a child. It is not punishment. It is liberating. Children who learn the value of earning money from a young age are going to be so far ahead of the curve when they are out of school and on their own," Orman says. "Earning [their] own money, providing for [themselves], instills such a sense of pride and capability."[3]

on a used car. This amount was on top of the car loan she took out from the bank.

The reality was that Jasmine should have been saving money, not spending it. She had financial obligations, including upcoming college application fees. Jasmine planned to apply for financial aid at the colleges that accepted her. But she also needed to start putting away money for textbooks and other school supplies.

More importantly, Jasmine was already in debt and wasn't managing it properly. Instead of paying off her car loan responsibly and being frugal, she was adding even more debt by using her credit card for a spending spree on a party. If she kept it up, she'd be deep in

SPENDING PERSONALITY TYPES

People have different types of spending habits. For example, big spenders are people who spend money without thinking about the consequences. They're constantly broke and likely in debt. Strict savers are people who never shell out cash for any reason. Saving spenders are people who have a healthy attitude when it comes to spending money. They'll treat themselves on special occasions, but they know when to call it quits. While thriftiness is always a good idea, spending some money is acceptable every once in a while. A middle-of-the-road approach is a smart way to avoid unnecessary debt while also enjoying the experiences that money can buy.

debt by the time she graduated high school. How would she be able to manage? Jasmine needed to rethink her relationship with money.

EXCESS SPENDING AND DEBT

Situations like Jasmine's aren't uncommon. Purchasing items can be done easily online with the click of a mouse. That ease makes it even more challenging to control spending and avoid going into debt.

According to experts, spending a little money each month is rarely a problem if a person has enough money in the bank.

But excessive shopping binges can lead to borrowing or taking out a line of credit. Too much borrowing can lead to debt. Once someone gets into debt, it can be difficult to get out.

For many teens and adults, managing money can seem overwhelming at times. But understanding what debt is, why it occurs, and how to prevent it from happening is important in being financially responsible. If debt becomes a problem, there are ways to manage the situation. Understanding what credit is, how debt affects credit potential, and how to pay off debt also helps people stay on track financially for the long term.

WHAT'S YOUR ATTITUDE TOWARD SPENDING?

Before you learn about what debt and its effects are, it's a good idea to assess your attitude toward spending. It can help you figure out how you might handle money and debt in the future.

1. It's your birthday and time to celebrate. Which party-planning approach do you take?

    a. Definitely Jasmine's. Dinner, dancing, bonfire, the works. Sure, money's tight. But we only live once, right?

    b. A potluck with friends, where everyone brings a home-cooked dish or snack. I'm saving for a new winter jacket and want to make sure I have enough to cover the cost.

2. Last month, you borrowed $50 from your best friend. When do you pay him back?

    a. A month? A few months? Who knows? My friend won't care. Borrowing money is what friends are for.

    b. As soon as I can. Owing money to a good friend is OK in the short term, but it's important to repay debt as soon as possible. Plus, taking advantage of my friend's goodwill isn't something I want to get in the habit of doing.

3. When you read the phrase "money management," your first thought is:

   a. Super boring. Keeping track of expenses can't be that important.
   b. Sometimes confusing, but very important. Learning how to become money smart is the key to success.

If most of your answers were "a," you may not have the best attitude when it comes to money. What's more, you might even be in debt. If most of your answers were "b," you tend to act responsibly when it comes to spending and saving. While you might have a little debt on your plate, there's a healthy chance you also have a plan for taking care of it.

CHAPTER TWO

SLOPPY SPENDING

On April 13, 2018, an article in *Money* magazine had an attention-getting first sentence: "Americans have fallen back in love with debt."[1] The article went on to report the average amount of debt people in the United States held at every age in 2017. According to a study of consumer finances commissioned by the Federal Reserve Bank of New York, the total US household debt had reached $13 trillion—the highest ever recorded. People between the ages of 45 and 54 had the most debt overall, totaling an average of $134,600. People ages 75 and older had the lowest amount, at $34,500. Somewhere in the middle were people younger than 35. They averaged $67,400 in debt.[2]

This amount of debt isn't uncommon. In fact, according to a 2018 study from Comet, a financial services company, 80.9 percent of Americans between the ages of 54 and 72 are in debt. About 79.9 percent

Some people buy items that are wants instead of needs, such as expensive boats.

A LONG HISTORY OF DEBT

Debt seems like a modern concept. But it has actually been around for thousands of years. According to David Graeber, author of *Debt: The First 5,000 Years*, people were in debt as early as 3500 BCE. The most common debt tool was a stick. When a debt was owed, a notch was etched into the stick. Then the stick was broken in half. The section the debtor kept was called the stub. The creditor kept the other half, known as the stock.

of people between 38 and 53 are in debt. And about 81.5 percent of people between 22 and 37 are in debt.[3]

Many economists ask why so many people live beyond their means. In truth, there are many reasons—some good, others bad. For example, most people don't have enough cash on hand to pay for a house, so they take out a mortgage. A mortgage is a legal agreement allowing someone to borrow money from a bank or similar organization to buy a home. This is an example of good debt. Other people take out loans or use payment plans to buy a second car, a boat, or some other object they might want, but don't necessarily need. This could be an example of bad debt. Medical bills, credit card usage, and student loans are all ways someone can rack up both good and bad debt.

GENERATIONAL DEBT[4]

People have debt for many reasons. In 2018, Comet released a survey of 1,000 people showing the amount of debt three generations of people have in the United States. These generations are baby boomers (born between 1946 and 1964), Generation X (born between 1965 and 1980), and millennials (born between 1981 and 1997).

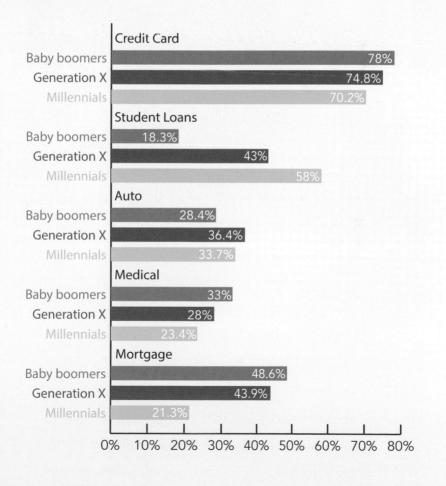

Credit Card
- Baby boomers: 78%
- Generation X: 74.8%
- Millennials: 70.2%

Student Loans
- Baby boomers: 18.3%
- Generation X: 43%
- Millennials: 58%

Auto
- Baby boomers: 28.4%
- Generation X: 36.4%
- Millennials: 33.7%

Medical
- Baby boomers: 33%
- Generation X: 28%
- Millennials: 23.4%

Mortgage
- Baby boomers: 48.6%
- Generation X: 43.9%
- Millennials: 21.3%

0% 10% 20% 30% 40% 50% 60% 70% 80%

Gaming devices can cost hundreds of dollars.

NEEDS VS. WANTS

Debt can happen to anyone, no matter their age, gender, race, religion, cultural background, or social class. One of the biggest overarching contributors to bad debt for young adults is sloppy spending. "The simplest explanation is that debt happens when you spend more than you earn," says US Chamber of Commerce Foundation personal finance writer

Tim Lemke.[5] This often occurs when a person doesn't know the difference between a need and a want.

For example, college student Jaquan has been eyeing the Sony PlayStation 4 Pro for months. It costs about $400 new. For years, Jaquan has played video games on an old Xbox. But all of his friends have the new PlayStation, and he thinks he needs to keep up with the latest trends. The only problem is that Jaquan doesn't have the money to buy the system. He uses his credit card to buy the system and a few new games. In the short term, he's incredibly happy. But problems arise when Jaquan doesn't have enough money that month to pay both his rent and his credit card bill. Just one purchase can lead to debt.

For Jaquan, the video game console was clearly a want, not a need— although it might have felt like a need to him. So what's the difference? A need is something

WANTS AND NEEDS

According to Leslie H. Tayne, founder of a debt relief law firm in New York, needs and wants aren't the same for everyone. One person's want might be another person's need. For example, Sasha might need a laptop for school because he doesn't have one. But for Cullen, who already has a desktop and a tablet, a new laptop might just be a luxury. "Can that person live without that item? Is it absolutely necessary . . . ?" Tayne asks.[6] If not, it's a want.

HOW TO PRIORITIZE?

Sometimes borrowing money is unavoidable. But to avoid insurmountable debt, people must first categorize their needs and wants and then take a critical look at their needs. Finance reporter Courtney Jespersen suggests looking for less expensive ways to meet needs. For example, call the phone company and ask for a different monthly plan. Or move the list of needs and wants around. "Take a close look at your categories. Some of the items you've indicated as needs may actually be wants, or vice versa," she writes.[7]

a person must have to live and work healthfully and efficiently. Housing, food, transportation, electricity, and clothing are all needs in most people's lives.

Wants are expenses that help people enjoy their day-to-day lives and live in a more comfortable manner. They are things such as vacations, music and books, gym memberships, and designer clothes. It's possible to survive without them.

To avoid debt, it's important to know the difference between needs and wants and plan a budget accordingly. For example, daily meals are necessary, but morning lattes at the coffee cart aren't. In Jaquan's case, he should have prioritized his needs. Instead, he gave in to his wants, which led to debt.

People should think carefully before buying expensive items.

IRRESPONSIBLE SPENDING

In addition to not knowing the difference between needs and wants, another leading cause of debt is simply not caring about the difference and spending money anyway. This type of excessive behavior can take many forms. Many people are prone to making impulse purchases to keep up with friends or family. For example, they see a flashy new flat-screen television while shopping for a toaster and, without really thinking about whether they can afford it, add the TV to their cart.

"No one is implying you don't deserve to treat yourself to nice things or vacations once in a while; but if you can't actually afford those things, what favors are you doing yourself?" writes Lemke. "The spiral into debt can be quick and overwhelming. Showing off isn't worth your financial wellbeing."[8]

Another irresponsible behavior—one with even darker undertones—is when shopping becomes compulsive. People who are compulsive shoppers can't resist the urge to spend money on items or services, whether or not they're necessary. Sometimes this behavior is mixed with feelings of guilt or depression. Other times it can lead to criminal behavior, such as stealing. More often than not, compulsive shoppers rack up huge amounts of debt they can't pay back.

But shopping doesn't always lead to poor financial decisions. Not all debt is considered bad, either. In fact, in many situations— especially for younger people just starting out in life—picking up certain kinds of debt is considered a smart choice on the path to creating an independent, financially grounded future.

SHOPAHOLICS ANONYMOUS

For most people, shopping is a fun, occasional opportunity to buy new stuff. But for others, shopping can be a debilitating addiction. According to the Shulman Center for Compulsive Theft, Spending, and Hoarding, between 5 and 9 percent of Americans have compulsive shopping disorders.[9] Luckily, support groups are available to help them, including Shopaholics Anonymous and Debtors Anonymous. Each offers one-on-one, phone, chat, or in-person group meetings. Another option is meeting with a certified financial professional to get spending back on track.

FIGURING OUT YOUR NEEDS AND WANTS

Understanding the difference between needs and wants is important in avoiding debt accumulation. Think about your life. What are your needs? What are your wants? How are they similar or different?

NEEDS	WANTS

After you're done, look at your list. See if anything you listed as a need can be reclassified as a want to help cut spending or debt. Pick one need and write about why making it a want might be better for your finances.

_____

_____

_____

_____

_____

_____

_____

_____

_____

_____

_____

_____

_____

_____

_____

_____

_____

CHAPTER THREE

GOOD DEBT

F or a small number of people, living debt-free is doable. But it's not always the right choice. In fact, most people in the United States don't have enough cash to buy everything they want. But the good news is that many financial experts say that's perfectly fine. They believe carrying some debt is actually a smart idea—as long as the debt is the responsible kind.

But what exactly is responsible debt? "Good debt is an investment that will grow in value or generate long-term income," says financial reporter Dave Roos.[1] To understand Roos's point more clearly, think about the following example. Alejandra and her family moved from New York City to rural Oregon. In New York, Alejandra could take the subway anywhere she wanted to go. But now that she lives in the country, she doesn't have a way to get around. She could borrow the family's car, but her mother uses it for work.

A home mortgage is considered good debt.

Even with a full-time job, many people can't afford to purchase an expensive item, such as a car, outright.

Alejandra has an after-school job bagging groceries at the local supermarket. Still, she doesn't have enough money to buy a car with cash, even a cheap one. But using the money she saved from her job, plus a little help from her parents, she made a down payment and took out a loan for a used car. Although she was a little worried about being able to pay it back, she believed the loan was a step in a positive direction. "An auto loan is [an] example of good debt, particularly if the

HOW LOANS WORK

A loan is a contract between a borrower and a lender. It stipulates the terms under which a sum of money borrowed must be repaid. Loans are taken out for a variety of reasons, including buying a car, paying for college, or starting a business.

Here's how loans generally work. Once people take out a loan, they agree to pay it back over a set period of time. Every month, the borrower pays back a portion of the loan until the balance is zero. The borrower is also responsible for paying interest—an additional fee charged by the lender that is usually a percentage of the principal. The principal is the total amount of money borrowed minus the payments that have already been made. If a person defaults, or doesn't make a payment, on the loan, the interest rate could increase. Additional fines could also be tacked on to the debt total.

vehicle is essential to doing business," says Roos, who also offers a caution. "[But], cars and trucks lose value over time, so it's in the buyer's best interest to pay as much as possible up front so as not to spend too much on high-interest monthly payments."[2]

By taking out the loan, Alejandra took on some debt. But because the car will help her get to and from school and work and make life generally easier for her and her family, the loan is considered a good debt. Alejandra was also smart because she paid enough money up front to keep her monthly payments affordable.

THE AVERAGE PRICE OF COLLEGE

College in the United States can be expensive, depending on the school. According to the College Board, an organization that helps prepare students for college, the average cost of college tuition and room and board for the 2018–2019 academic year was $21,370 for a four-year, in-state public school. It was $48,510 for a four-year private school located either in or out of state.[5] Before deciding on a college education, students must consider the overall cost of a higher education and what types of jobs are available after graduation. Loans can provide a boost as long as they are repaid. Grants and other merit-based scholarships gifted by charitable organizations, nonprofits, and other groups are another option. Grants don't have to be repaid.

STUDENT LOANS

One of the most common types of good debt for younger people is a college loan. In fact, 70 percent of people who graduated from college in 2018 took out some type of loan to pay for their education.[3] At first glance, this might seem like a terrible idea. After all, in 2016 the average monthly student loan payment was $393— and that's on top of paying for other needs such as groceries, rent, and transportation.[4]

Is a college loan really worth going into debt? It depends. In 2018, the average

College classes can cost thousands of dollars.

student loan debt for a person who graduated from college was more than $37,000.[6] A small number of people owe as much as $100,000 or more. According to *Forbes* magazine, 44 million people in the United States collectively hold nearly $1.5 trillion in student debt.[7] A large amount of debt can complicate the process of becoming financially independent after college graduation.

But the truth is that most US families can't afford the price of a higher education. Therefore, taking out a loan—and going into debt—is an investment in the future. It improves the chances of getting a job with a decent salary, health insurance, and retirement benefits. At the very least, it will provide college graduates with the knowledge and connections they need to move ahead in life. Plus, a college education is necessary in some fields. The Georgetown Center on Education and the Workforce reports that by 2020, 65 percent of all jobs in the US economy will require education beyond high school.[8] Fortunately,

TYPES OF COLLEGE LOANS

Many types of loans are available for students who want to attend college. Federal Direct Subsidized Loans don't accrue interest while the borrower is in college. They also have a borrowing limit. Federal Direct Unsubsidized Loans aren't need based. They have borrowing limits, flexible repayment terms, and low, fixed interest rates. Both subsidized and unsubsidized loans have income-driven terms that help protect borrowers. Federal Direct PLUS Loans allow parents of students to borrow the total cost of college, subtracting any financial aid received. State loans are also available in some states, and private loans are available in many places.

most federal student loans have income-driven repayment options that help protect borrowers if they don't do as well financially as they expected.

MORTGAGES

According to the Federal Reserve, the US central banking system, Americans collectively carried more than $15.1 trillion in mortgage debt as of September 2018.[9] That seems like a shocking figure. But aside from college loans, mortgages are considered by financial experts to be one of the most accepted forms of good debt.

A mortgage is beneficial because it allows a person to buy a home—even if he or she doesn't have the cash to pay for it. For example, if a house costs $375,000 and Mateo has only $50,000 saved, he may pay the $50,000 as a down payment and take out a loan to pay the remaining $325,000. The loan for $325,000 is Mateo's mortgage. Making mortgage payments is a bit like paying rent, but different. If Mateo was only renting the house, he would make monthly payments to a landlord or the owner of the house. As long as he made the payments in full and on time, he could stay in the house. Once he stopped paying, however, he'd have to leave. He would own nothing for the money he spent on rent. A mortgage

requires Mateo to make monthly payments and pay down his loan. But when he's finished with the payments, he'll actually own his house.

Mortgages are usually long-term loans. The most common mortgages run for either 15 or 30 years. They have lower interest rates than other types of debt. "[This allows] you to keep the rest of your money free for investments and emergencies," writes Roos. "The ideal situation would be that your home increases in market value over time, enough to cancel out the interest you've paid over that same period."[10]

UNDERSTANDING LOAN REPAYMENT FEES

In some situations, dealing with loan fees can lead to greater debt. Before taking out a loan, watch out for the following four offenders. Loan origination fees are charges a creditor uses to process the application for the loan. A failed payment fee is charged when there isn't enough money in a borrower's bank account to cover a payment. A late payment fee occurs when a payment is late. And some lenders even charge prepayment fees for paying a loan off early. That's because most lenders prefer to receive the full amount of interest from borrowers.

If people stop making payments on their mortgage, the house goes into foreclosure and is taken away from them.

SMALL BUSINESS LOANS

Another example of good debt is a small business loan. Someone just starting out as a freelancer or the owner of a new business needs all the help he or she can get. Employee salaries and health care, equipment and supplies, and the other costs of running a business can get expensive. Small business loans help owners handle those costs.

Many small business loan options are available. Business owners can apply for funding from banks, a microloan program that lends out small sums of money with low interest rates, or from the US Small Business Administration (SBA). Applicants need a

YOUNG ENTREPRENEURS AT THE SBA

Most small business loans are geared toward adults. But some resources are available to teens who want to become entrepreneurs. The US Small Business Administration (SBA) runs a free online course on its website that teaches young people about the ins and outs of running a business. The 30-minute course covers how to choose the best financing options available and how to legally register a business. The course also discusses how to conduct market research and provides tips on creating a solid business plan. The website also has a full transcript of the course.

strong business credit score to be considered. They must also have a detailed business plan explaining the business's purpose, operation, and revenue and expense projections for the next five years.

But like any loan situation, a smart loan repayment plan is crucial to prevent debt from harming the business's future success. Shopping around for the best rates is also important. "No matter the source of your financing, you should only seek a loan if you're experiencing a [gap in your cash flow]," says personal finance reporter Damian Davilla. "There are several financing options available, so don't jump at the first loan offer that you receive."[11]

WHAT IS GOOD DEBT?

Test your knowledge of good debt by answering the following multiple-choice questions.

1. If you want to buy a house but need help making the payments, you would take out which of the following?

   a. A mortgage

   b. A Federal Perkins loan

   c. A Federal Direct PLUS grant

2. If you want to start a business but don't have enough cash to do so, it's better to do which of the following?

   a. Take out a small business loan

   b. Put all the charges on a credit card

   c. Don't start a business if you don't have enough money

3. When is taking out a car loan considered an example of good debt?

   a. Any time—owning a car is a great way to build credit even if you don't need it

   b. Never—taking out a car loan is always considered bad debt

c. Sometimes—if you need the car for school or work and can make the payments on time, it's good debt

4. If you want to make the most financially responsible decision when relocating to a new home, you should do which of the following?

   a. Take out a mortgage to buy a home
   b. Save money by renting a house, and then rent another house when you can't afford the first one anymore
   c. Don't do either, and instead rely on friends and family to house and support you

Answer key: 1) a; 2) a; 3) c; 4) a

Borrowing money for some things is OK, but have a plan to pay it back.

CHAPTER FOUR

BAD DEBT

Some people think all debt should be considered bad debt, but that's not necessarily true. College loans and mortgages are great examples of debts that help people grow toward a positive future. Some debts, such as car loans, may be considered good or bad, depending on whether the benefits are worthwhile and the balance is paid off each month. However, some debts always fall into the bad category. These types of financial transactions are either for items that quickly lose their value or those that don't generate long-term income.

Consider the following example. Maren lives in Montana. She loves to read, paint, and write poetry. Her friends are active. They go on multiday backpacking trips into the wilderness, sometimes camping for days in the Rocky Mountains. Maren doesn't care for sleeping outdoors, but when her friend invites her to a weeklong trip during spring

Credit card debt is considered bad debt.

break, Maren accepts. However, she doesn't have any camping gear. So a few days before the trip, she buys a brand-new tent, hiking boots, hiking poles, hiking pants, a rain jacket, sleeping bag, sleeping pad, and a backpack. The total price for these items is more than $1,000.

AVOID DEBT BY BEING THRIFTY

Piling up charges on designer clothes or other unnecessary items is never a good idea because it can quickly lead to debt accumulation. But buying the occasional treat is OK every once in a while—as long as it's a smart purchase. Instead of buying new items, some people choose to shop at places such as thrift stores instead. Bargain hunting for used clothes, books, camping gear, and even furniture is usually cheaper than buying new. However, the quality may not be as good as new items.

Maren doesn't have cash to pay for all her new gear, so she charges the purchases to her credit card. She realizes that she'll probably never use any of the camping stuff again, and it may take her a few months to pay off the debt. But she's excited to spend time with her friends on spring break. And she figures that she can always sell some of the stuff online or at the local pawnshop if she gets desperate.

Most financial experts would agree that Maren is accumulating bad debt—especially because she doesn't have money in her bank account to support it. "The general rule to avoid bad debt is: If you can't afford it and you don't need it, don't buy it," says Dave Roos. "If you buy a fancy, $200 pair of shoes on your credit card, but can't pay the balance on your card for years, those shoes will eventually cost you over $250, and by then they'll be out of style."[1]

PAYDAY LOANS

One of the worst examples of bad debt is a payday loan. Few teenagers will come across these loans in their daily lives, but it's important to know what they are in case the

THE DIRT ON PAWNSHOPS

For some people, pawnshops are an easy solution when managing debt. They bring an item into a shop and receive a fraction of the item's value as a cash loan. They then have one to four months to pay back the loan, plus interest and fees. In the meantime, the shop keeps the item until the borrower pays back the loan he or she received in full, including interest. But pawnshops are only a good idea if the borrower knows the value of his or her item and can bargain for a good price. Pawnshops have other downsides, too. Interest rates vary from 30 to 300 percent.[2] If the person can't pay back the loan, the pawnshop keeps the item and can sell it.

situation arises. Payday loans are short-term loans for small amounts of money that need to be repaid during the next paycheck cycle. In other words, they're a quick fix similar to a cash advance—a short-term cash loan taken against a credit card's credit line—with a really high interest rate.

Here's how payday loans work. Sloane has been out sick from work for two weeks. He's a month late on his rent and needs to pay his landlord. He doesn't have the money, so he goes to a payday lender and asks to borrow $500. In return, he writes the lender a postdated check for the amount he's borrowing, plus an interest fee of 15 percent, or $75. At the end of the loan's term, which coincides with his next paycheck, the lender deposits Sloane's check.

LOAN CALCULATORS

When evaluating debt risk, loans, and credit cards, doing the math and factoring in interest rates can be time consuming. But the good news is that most banks, financial organizations, and loan retailers offer loan calculators to consumers that figure these calculations. The loan calculators are usually available on the financial institution's website.

Some people who find themselves in a tight financial spot resort to getting a payday loan.

PAYDAY LOANS: THE DOWNWARD SPIRAL

According to the Pew Charitable Trusts, a nonprofit and nongovernmental organization that works to improve public policy, 12 million people in the United States take out payday loans each year. In doing so, they spend close to $9 billion on loan fees.[3] For people who are in a tight spot financially, payday loans may seem like a good idea and an easy fix. But many financial experts insist these loans are more like a trap if the initial payment isn't made immediately. If more than one loan is needed, interest payments can pile up while the original balance remains unpaid. Debt can double and even quadruple. "The problem is that the borrower usually needs to take another payday loan to pay off the first one. The whole reason for taking the first payday loan was that they didn't have the money for an emergency need. Since regular earnings will be consumed by regular expenses, they won't be any better off in two weeks," writes reporter Kevin Mercadante on the website MoneyUnder30.com. "A payday loan may seem like the only option in a financial emergency if you have poor credit and no savings. But it can do a LOT more harm than good."[4]

In theory, the situation would work and Sloane would just be penalized $75, the accumulated interest, on top of the loan. But most payday loan lenders charge an astronomical interest rate—as much as 500 percent or more—because they know the borrowers are in a tight spot. "What makes it even more concerning is the fact that it is the interest rate being charged to the people who can least afford it," writes financial reporter Kevin Mercadante. "If a person doesn't have $500 today, they probably won't be any more likely to have $575 in two weeks. But that's what they'll have to come up with. And that's why it gets worse."[5] In Sloane's case, each time he can't pay off the payday loan, the amount he owes increases exponentially, which leads to more and more debt.

CREDIT CARD DEBT

Perhaps the most widespread culprit in the bad debt category is credit card debt. According to NerdWallet—a personal finance website that analyzes data from the US Census Bureau, US Bureau of Labor Statistics, and US Federal Reserve—48 percent of all US households had some form of credit card debt in 2018.[6] The average household carried a balance of $15,482 in 2017.[7]

As with most financial services, problems arise not with having a credit card but with not paying off the balance on time. Each month a balance isn't paid off, interest is tacked on to the total. "There's nothing inherently wrong with using a credit card; the problem is when you don't pay off the balance," said NerdWallet credit card and banking expert Kimberly Palmer. "Because the interest is so high, it can snowball

TOP CONTRIBUTORS TO CREDIT CARD DEBT[8]

In November 2017, NerdWallet surveyed 2,089 adults, including 1,201 with credit card debt, about their spending habits. NerdWallet wanted to pinpoint the biggest contributors to credit card debt. The study asked participants to pick a few of the top reasons why their spending got out of control out of a list of provided factors. Forty-one percent chose spending an unaffordable amount on unnecessary purchases.

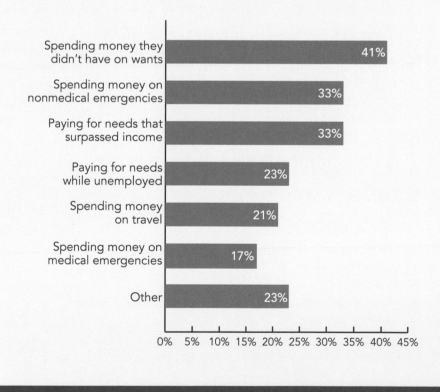

Category	Percentage
Spending money they didn't have on wants	41%
Spending money on nonmedical emergencies	33%
Paying for needs that surpassed income	33%
Paying for needs while unemployed	23%
Spending money on travel	21%
Spending money on medical emergencies	17%
Other	23%

0% 5% 10% 15% 20% 25% 30% 35% 40% 45%

so quickly." Estimates show the average US household paid $1,292 in interest on credit card debt in 2017.[9]

However, not all credit cards are created equal. Some offer rewards, points, or airline miles. These bonuses can make these cards a better deal for their holders if people pay off the balance every month. Many financial experts consider these cards more beneficial for consumers. Other cards have high interest rates. If a cardholder doesn't pay off the credit card balance each month, he or she could fall into debt. When considering a credit card, it's always best to do research before signing up to avoid any financial pitfalls that could lead to debt.

GOOD DEBT OR BAD DEBT?

Test your understanding of the difference between good debt and bad debt. Decide between "good" and "bad" for each scenario below.

1. All of Suki's friends in high school have cars, and Suki wants one, too. She doesn't have the money to pay for it, so she takes out an auto loan, even though the public transportation system in her hometown of San Francisco, California, is excellent.

   GOOD   BAD

2. Marshan dreams of becoming an artist, but he needs more education. He wants to apply to Parsons School of Design in New York City, but he needs some financial aid. He applies for a scholarship and a federal loan so he can get his degree in fine arts.

   GOOD   BAD

3. Kimberly needs some quick cash, so she goes to the pawnshop. She gets a quick loan to buy a laptop computer and a pair of designer shoes.

   GOOD   BAD

4. Norma and Ed just got married and want to start a family. But they live in a small apartment in Brooklyn, New York. One weekend, they take a trip to New Jersey and find a beautiful house. They'll have to take out a mortgage, but they're ready to take the plunge.

GOOD   **BAD**

5. Roberto wants to be in a band, but he doesn't have any instruments. He also doesn't know what instrument he wants to play. On a whim, he decides to buy a brand-new set of drums. He goes to a local shop and takes out a payday loan so he can get enough cash to buy the drum set.

GOOD   **BAD**

Answer key: 1) Bad; 2) Good; 3) Bad; 4) Good; 5) Bad

CHAPTER FIVE

THE LOWDOWN ON CREDIT CARDS

C redit cards can have many disadvantages. Impulse shopping can lead to overspending, which can lead to a mammoth credit card bill, which turns into debt if the balance isn't paid off. But using credit cards correctly also has advantages. For one, they provide a helpful record of spending through monthly statements and online accounts. Most offer purchase protection on charges. Credit cards also offer users an easy way to build good credit as long as the full balance is paid on time each month. Good or bad credit is partially dependent on how people handle their credit card bills.

Before covering the different types of credit cards, it's important first to understand how most credit cards work. All credit cards have credit limits. This figure tells

Credit cards are often convenient to use while shopping.

CREDIT CARDS VS. DEBIT CARDS

Credit cards and debit cards may look the same, but they're not. With debit cards, users buy something and pay for it right away. The funds are automatically subtracted from the user's checking account, so no interest is charged. Some fees involved occur if a user charges more money on the debit card than is available in the checking account. This is called an overdraft fee. On one hand, debit cards are easier to use than writing a check. But users must make sure they already have the funds to pay for their purchases.

Credit cards operate under the rules of buy now, pay later. Charges are applied if the credit card holder carries a balance or incurs interest charges. Fees can also be imposed if payments aren't made on time. Some credit cards also have annual fees. On the positive side, many credit cards offer incentives such as cash back, points, or travel rewards. But it's also much easier to acquire debt by using a credit card than it is using a debit card.

a consumer how much he or she is allowed to charge. The limit is based on a person's ability to handle debt. For example, if a person never pays his or her bills on time and doesn't make much money, the credit limit will probably be low. First-time credit card holders have low credit limits, too.

Every credit card has an interest rate attached to it. This fee, called the annual percentage rate (APR), is charged whenever the credit card holder doesn't

Some people struggle to pay off their credit card debt.

pay the card's balance in full when it is due. According to the financial website the Mint, credit card rates can be as low as 18 percent or as high as 24 percent, depending on the cardholder's credit history.[1] Some card companies also give promotional rates for a certain amount of time. Many offer an introductory 0 percent APR for the first year to attract customers. But if the credit card owner misses even one payment, the interest rate increases.

Though they aren't required, most credit cards also have a grace period. This is a window of time between the end of a billing cycle and the date the payment is due. If a payment on the outstanding balance isn't paid by the due date, the company charges the cardholder interest on the unpaid portion of the balance. The company will also charge a late fee, which can be as much as $35.[2] Interest on purchases in the new billing cycle, beginning on the date each purchase is made, also accumulates. Therefore, it's best to pay off credit card bills in full each month by the due date to avoid late charges and interest fees.

SECURED CREDIT CARDS

Many types of credit cards exist, most of which aren't available to teens. But one option teens do have is the secured credit card, which is reserved for people with either poor credit or no credit. In order to secure the line of credit, secured credit cards require the cardholder to put down a deposit. The credit limit on the card is usually equal to the amount of that deposit.

For example, Brandy is 18 and doesn't have any credit history. She signs up for a secured credit card and puts down a $1,000 deposit. With the card, she can charge up to $1,000. But if she closes the account without paying off the card, she doesn't get her deposit back. "Secured credit cards are typically limited in their reward offerings, but they can be a good option for those looking to rebuild or establish credit," writes Credit Karma financial reporter Melanie Lockert.[3]

WHAT'S AN ANNUAL FEE?

Many credit cards are free to use as long as they are paid off in full on time. But some cards have an annual fee. This may be because the card offers some type of benefit to the user. For example, the Chase Sapphire Reserve card is one of the most popular credit cards, according to NerdWallet. Cardholders earn three points for every dollar they spend, and they can redeem those points on travel-related purchases. Plus, they get a $300 annual credit for things such as airline tickets or hotels. But the card costs $450 per year.[4] When choosing a credit card with an annual fee, it's important to consider whether the benefits outweigh the costs.

BECOME AN AUTHORIZED USER

Most unsecured credit cards are only available to people 21 and older, but younger people do have an option. Teens can become authorized users on their parent or guardian's credit card account.

Another option Brandy has is a student credit card. This type of starter card is for college students who have little to no credit history. They come with a low credit limit but are usually easier to get approved for than other credit cards.

Some require a deposit but also have a low annual fee or no fee at all. "Credit cards that teens can get typically have pretty high regular interest rates," writes WalletHub financial reporter John Kiernan. "So it's important for teens to pay their credit card bills both on time and in full every month. This will help [them] save money and allow [their] credit score to improve."[5]

UNSECURED CREDIT CARDS

Unsecured credit cards are the most common type of card available. These are usually reserved for people with good or excellent credit, although consumers with less than stellar credit can usually obtain one at a higher interest rate and low credit limit. Unsecured credit cards don't require a user to put down a cash deposit for security.

Consumers have many options when it comes to choosing the right unsecured credit card for their lifestyle. Travel rewards credit cards usually partner with airlines or hotels and offer cardholders airline miles or points that can be redeemed for travel-related purposes. Gas rewards credit cards offer cash back when paying at the gas pump. Retail credit cards allow users to earn points for products purchased from a particular retailer, such as a department store or online retailer.

Cash-conscious cardholders may prefer cash-back cards. They give a percentage of money back to cardholders on eligible purchases. "This type of credit

PROMOTIONAL SIGN-UP BONUSES

Many credit cards offer a promotional deal to attract new customers at different times of the year. Typical sign-up bonuses require the cardholder to spend a certain amount within the first few months of opening the account before the reward kicks in. Bonuses usually come in the form of points, miles, cash back, or a statement credit. For example, the Delta SkyMiles American Express card sometimes offers a flight mile bonus to users who spend thousands of dollars within a set number of months. However, if the user doesn't spend the amount, he or she doesn't get the reward.

PREPAID CARDS AND GIFT CARDS

Prepaid cards look like credit cards, but they aren't the same thing. Instead, they are purchased at a store with cash, a debit card, or a credit card. Some prepaid cards can only be used in certain stores, such as department stores. These are commonly known as gift cards. Others can be used anywhere and are refilled with cash when the balance runs out. Prepaid cards are convenient because they aren't attached to a bank account and only have a fixed balance. But some have hidden fees or complex terms and conditions. Plus, if a prepaid card gets lost or stolen, the money on the card is lost as well.

card is a good option for budget-savvy cardholders looking to get the most bang for their buck," says Lockert.[6]

Credit cards offer flexibility for people who may not have enough cash on hand to make a purchase. In addition, they allow people to shop online and provide some protections against fraud. They're also a great way to stock up on things such as airline miles or hotel rewards points. And as with any type of loans, staying on top of bill payments is essential to steer clear of debt.

"The easiest way to live beyond your means is to have a pocket full of credit cards," writes Christine Romans, author of *Smart is the New Rich: Money*

Many people use their credit cards to shop online.

Missing credit card payments isn't good for a person's credit score.

Guide for Millennials. "[But] if you want to build a credit history and know that you will pay the balance off every month, a credit card is a valuable tool for you. It is critical that you pay the balance every month and not use it to float from paycheck to paycheck or to live above your means."[7]

CARD COMPARISON

If you were going to get a credit card and pay it off in full, which one would you choose and why? Use an internet search engine to research three different credit card options you might consider. Fill in the chart with any details you find. Ask an adult for help if you need further assistance.

	Credit Card #1	Credit Card #2	Credit Card #3
Name of Credit Card			
What is the APR?			
Introductory APR?			
Penalty APR?			
What are the fees?			
Annual fee?			
Late fee?			
Over-the-limit fee?			
Other fees?			
Are there any benefits?			
Airline miles?			
Rewards points?			
Cash back?			
Gas rewards?			
Other rewards?			
Is there a grace period?			
Is the card . . . ?			
Secured?			
Unsecured?			
Authorized user on parent or guardian's account?			
Prepaid?			
Student card?			
Other starter card?			
What are the other benefits?			
Excellent customer service?			
Easy-to-use website?			
Local office?			

CHAPTER SIX

BUILDING GOOD CREDIT

C redit seems like a simple concept. For example, Brooke doesn't have the money to buy the new bike he wants. He puts the charge on his credit card and pays the balance off after he gets his next paycheck from work.

But the process of building and maintaining good credit is a little more complicated than that. In fact, a person's credit history depends on factors other than paying bills on time. It's also used as a measurement tool in other situations, such as new employee or renter background checks. Understanding how credit works is one of the most important aspects of becoming a financially independent and responsible adult.

Credit scores show whether people have good or bad credit.

WHAT IS A CREDIT SCORE?

Everyone who takes out credit or borrows money is assigned a credit score. A credit score is basically a report card of how people handle their finances. Do they overspend? Do they pay their bills on time? This information is tracked and sent to credit bureaus from banks, credit card or loan companies, and even utility companies.

In the United States, three major credit bureaus monitor a person's credit history: Experian, TransUnion, and Equifax. These agencies then send their reports to the Fair Isaac Corporation (FICO), which assigns the person a three-digit number called a FICO score. This number is commonly called a credit score. As the person spends money and pays down his or her debt, the number goes up or down. The FICO score helps lenders determine what kind of credit risk people are likely to be and whether they will pay the money they owe. The higher the credit score, the lower the risk, and the more likely a lender will give that person credit at a low rate.

FICO scores usually range from 300 to 850. According to Experian, a score of 800 or higher means the person has fantastic financial habits. People with above-average credit usually have a credit score

BREAKDOWN OF FICO CREDIT SCORES[1]

According to Experian, more than one-half of Americans have a FICO score of good or better.

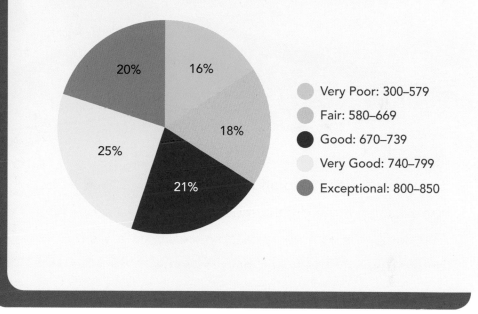

20% 16%

18%

25%

21%

- Very Poor: 300–579
- Fair: 580–669
- Good: 670–739
- Very Good: 740–799
- Exceptional: 800–850

between 740 and 799. Acceptable credit falls between 670 and 739. Below-average credit is from 580 to 669. Those who have a credit score of 579 or lower are high risk because they have a lot of debt and a poor repayment history.

FICO scores are a determining factor in many aspects of life. People with excellent scores have access to lower car insurance rates and lower interest

Credit scores affect interest rates on loans.

rates on small business loans and mortgages. People with bad scores because of late payments or no credit are seen as high risk by lenders. They are charged higher interest rates and might have a hard time getting loans.

"The scary fact is that the credit score is a three-digit number that could cost you—or save you—tens of thousands of dollars over a lifetime. It *is* scary, but my advice is: Don't obsess over this number," writes Christine Romans. "Pay your bills on time every time, slowly pay down your debt, and the score will rise. So don't ignore it, but don't obsess about it either."[2]

BUILDING AND KEEPING GOOD CREDIT

A few paths exist for teens looking to build their credit while staying out of debt. In the United States, a person must be at least 21 to apply for an unsecured credit card. But a starter credit card—the generic term for the types of cards available to students, first-time credit card owners, or those with little to no credit history—is an

THE CARD ACT

On May 22, 2009, President Barack Obama signed the Credit Card Accountability, Responsibility and Disclosure (CARD) Act into law. Among other rules, it restricted card issuance to some people under 21 years old, in part to help protect college students who were targeted by credit card companies prior to the law being passed. "The provision protects young people who lack the means or the knowledge to handle credit cards from miring themselves into debt," said Greg McBride, senior financial analyst at Bankrate.com.[3]

At the time, a study by student loan lending company Sallie Mae reported that college students carried an average balance of $3,173 on their credit cards. Furthermore, 82 percent of those students carried a balance from month to month, instead of paying it off each month.[4]

alternate option. According to WalletHub, teens can start by applying for a secured credit card geared specifically toward students.

If financial circumstances allow it, teens can take out a car loan and ask a parent or guardian to be a cosigner. This is another way to establish good credit without paying a deposit for a secured card. A third option for teens is to use a debit card attached to a bank account or credit union. After they turn 21, young adults can find a low-fee credit card and start using it to build credit.

Whether it's a loan or a credit card, the most important tip for teens and adults to remember is to pay bills on time to avoid any late fees. Setting up automatic payments is a way to make sure that happens. It's also important not to max out any credit cards. If possible, people should pay off any bills in full every month. Paying off the minimum amount will allow balances to carry over and incur more interest charges.

Credit experts recommend that both teens and adults keep the total charges on their credit card to less than 10 percent of the card's credit limit.[5] The ratio of how much credit people are using to how much they have available is called the credit utilization ratio. Sticking to a ratio of less than 10 percent makes it easier to pay off the card. For example, if a card has a

WHAT'S IN A CREDIT REPORT?

Patricia is interested in getting her credit checked for the first time to find out her FICO score. But she's not sure what to expect. What kind of information will be listed? Most credit reports contain a list of all the places a person has lived throughout his or her life. They also include the person's Social Security number, a list of current and previous employers, and estimated income.

In addition, Patricia's credit report will contain detailed information about each credit card account she has, including the type of account, any balance she owes, and her payment history. It also lists the loans she has, including the one she took out to buy her car and her student loans for four years of college. In addition, if Patricia had ever declared bankruptcy, that information would be on her credit report, too.

credit limit of $10,000, the cardholder should charge purchases of $1,000 or less a month. "If you routinely charge right up to your credit limit and pay it off, it looks less responsible than if you are just using some of your available credit each month. Especially if you are within a year of a major purchase—a car loan, for example—you should keep that credit utilization ratio low," suggests Romans.[6]

Finally, people should avoid opening up too many credit cards or getting too many loans at once. Though it might be tempting to capitalize on a travel credit card–related promotional bonus, submitting too many

People who max out a lot of credit cards can find themselves in serious debt.

credit applications will cause FICO scores to drop. "Applying for new credit accounts, such as department store cards or lines of credit can [account] for a small FICO score drop," says the FICO team. "Each time you apply for new credit, an 'inquiry' is added to your credit report. Each of these inquiries can have a small impact on your FICO score, and several inquiries in a short time frame will have a greater impact on your score than a single inquiry."[7]

TEST YOUR CREDIT SCORE KNOWLEDGE

Answer these true or false statements to see how much you know about how credit works.

1. The lower the score, the better your credit is. **True or False**

2. There are two major credit agencies that keep track of a person's credit history: Experian and Equifax. **True or False**

3. A poor credit score doesn't have much effect when it comes to getting hired for a job. Employers never check potential employees' credit reports. **True or False**

4. It's acceptable to open a bunch of credit card accounts at once. It won't affect your credit score. **True or False**

5. There are only three major factors that contribute to your credit score: the length of your credit history, how many credit cards you have, and how much you owe. **True or False**

Did you realize that the answers to all of these statements are false? It's important for you to identify inaccurate information that can impact your finances in the future.

CHAPTER SEVEN

PAYING DOWN DEBT

I magine the following scenario. Twenty-three-year-old Shayna is in a bit of a messy situation. She can't stop spending money, which has put her in a massive amount of debt. First, she maxed out her credit card, even though she couldn't afford to pay off the balance. She opened up another credit card because she needed money right away, but she put too many charges on that one, too. Then she got fired from her job. She's two months late on rent. She's also more than 270 days late on her student loan payments, which means they are in default, making her ineligible for deferment or debt forgiveness. Shayna feels worried and stuck. Her credit score has tanked. She wants to pay down her debt but doesn't know how. She needs help—fast.

Shayna's situation is very serious. It will take time to resolve. But she can use a few methods to slowly chip away at her debt and make the situation more

People who are in debt need a plan for how to get out of it.

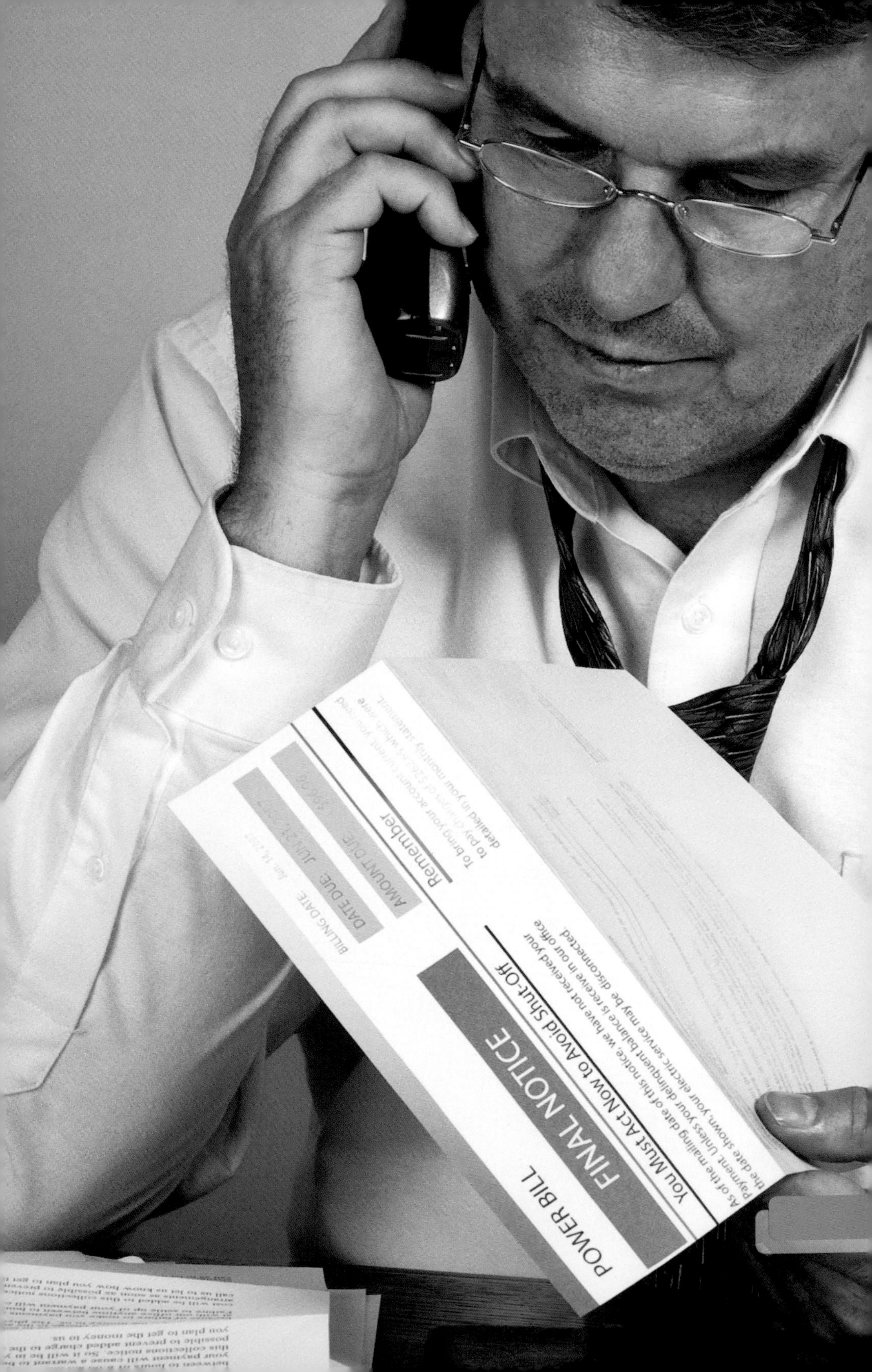

POWER BILL

FINAL NOTICE

You MUST Act Now to Avoid Shut-Off

As of the mailing date of this notice, we have not received your payment. Unless your delinquent balance is received in our office the date shown, your electric service may be disconnected

BILLING DATE   Jan. 14, 2007

DATE DUE   JUNE 21, 2007

AMOUNT DUE $94.00

Remember

To bring your account current when you pay. $226.00 is the amount due to pay Charges of detailed in your monthly statement.

manageable. One way is called debt laddering. If Shayna uses this approach, she'll make payments on the credit card or loan with the highest interest rate first. These payments would be significantly more than the minimum payment. At the same time, she would make minimum monthly payments on all of her other accounts. When the account with the highest interest rate is paid off completely, Shayna would then move on to the account with the next-highest rate. "This method will only work quickly if you stop using the accounts you are trying to pay off," says Tamsen Butler, a personal finance writer. "Otherwise, you will spend more time paying off your balances because you keep adding to them."[1]

Another option for Shayna is to use a similar approach to paying off her debts, but in reverse. Often called the debt-snowball method, it calls for starting with the account that has the smallest balance and paying that one off first. Shayna might rack up more interest charges if she chooses this route. But she'll also pay off more accounts at a faster rate.

"The idea is that quickly paying off accounts will keep you motivated and make you want to keep working toward paying off all your debt instead of

Not being able to pay important bills, such as utility bills, can put a lot of stress on people.

getting discouraged and giving up," says Butler. "After all, a huge part of managing your finances is psychological. If you can talk yourself into getting serious about paying down your debt, you will have a better chance of succeeding with your goal than if you only worked toward it half-heartedly."[2]

DEBT CONSOLIDATION

For people who have several debts, consolidating these debts into one payment is another way to tackle the problem. In some cases, the new consolidated debt will have a lower monthly interest rate. It will also make the repayment process easier because there's a way to track how much is owed in one place.

Banks, credit unions, and installment loan lenders offer debt consolidation loans. Most also provide debt management counseling to help clients develop

SELLING ASSETS

In addition to debt consolidation, people can sell some of their assets to help pay off debts. Adults sell things such as a second car, old furniture, and clothes they don't often wear. But teens can sell items, too. Garage sales are a great way to raise cash and get rid of clutter. Websites and online services offer selling opportunities as well. Before putting possessions up for sale, teens should ask an adult for help.

repayment plans with lower interest rates. Not all credit-counseling services are legitimate or looking out for people's best interests, however. "Some of them charge hidden fees, called 'voluntary contributions,' that can quickly get expensive," says Dave Roos. "Others are able to win lower interest rates only after purposefully defaulting on all of your loans and ruining your credit score."[3]

DECLARING BANKRUPTCY

READ THE FINE PRINT

Whether it's a credit offer or a new student loan, it's always important to read the fine print on any financial agreement, contract, or application. Sometimes credit card offers with a low interest rate are available only for short periods of time. After the introductory period, the rate rises exponentially. Cash advance fees can be higher than anticipated. In some situations, credit card companies can raise interest rates whenever they want. Knowing the exact fees, interest rates, and any other details in fine print is important to avoid getting swindled.

For most people like Shayna, getting out of debt takes many months and sometimes even years. The process is difficult but doable. But for a small portion of the population, the debt is insurmountable and more serious action must be taken. For only the worst cases, bankruptcy is a way to eliminate debts or repay them under court protection and supervision.

The most common types of bankruptcy are Chapter 7 and Chapter 13. In Chapter 7 bankruptcy, a person's unsecured debt—money owed for things such as credit card balances, medical bills, and services aside from student loans that aren't backed by a specific asset—is wiped clean. Any secured debt—debt that is backed by property, such as real estate or a car—that can't be maintained is usually sold to repay the lender. For example, if Shayna had a mortgage and couldn't make her payments, she would have to sell her house. The proceeds would go to the bank.

Chapter 13 bankruptcy works a little differently. First, the debtor has to present a plan to the court that describes how he or she will pay down debt over a period of up to five years. Then a counselor called a trustee collects

BANKRUPT CORPORATIONS

Individuals aren't the only ones who can declare bankruptcy. Corporations can, too. Due in part to a shift from brick-and-mortar shopping to online shopping, more than 15 retailers filed for bankruptcy in 2018. Among the most notable companies were Nine West, Toys"R"Us, Brookstone, Claire's, the Bon Ton stores, Remington Outdoors, and Sears.

Bankruptcy forms are found on a US government website.

the payments as they are made and gives them to any existing creditors. The downside is there are a few fees associated with Chapter 13. Initial filing fees can cost as much as $300 or more.[4] If the debtor hires a bankruptcy lawyer, the lawyer fees are at least a few thousand dollars. The trustee also gets an extra 10 percent off the top.[5] The advantage of Chapter 13 is that debtors can keep their assets while paying off what they owe.

A CHAPTER 13 BANKRUPTCY PLAN

Filing for Chapter 13 bankruptcy is complicated, with many factors involved. The plan takes many things into account, including the total amount of debt and monthly income and expenses.

Only people who have some type of income—either a salary from a job, unemployment compensation, or even Social Security payments—can apply for Chapter 13 bankruptcy. First, they have to submit a plan to the court. This plan must show proof of income for at least six months prior to filing for bankruptcy. It also must include a detailed list of all monthly expenses, such as utility bills, rent or mortgage payment, and even groceries.

Once the debtor submits a plan, all his or her creditors file a document explaining what the debtor owes, called a Proof of Claim. It lists both regular debts and priority debts. These debts must be repaid in full, such as income tax and child support. Chapter 13 bankruptcy usually lasts between three and five years. At the end of these monthly payments, any unsecured debts that haven't been repaid are forgiven.

For adults, payments such as child support, alimony, and student loan obligations aren't usually eliminated during bankruptcy proceedings. Taxes still have to be paid as well. There are also serious consequences. The debt burden goes away, but bankruptcy stays on a credit report for up to ten years. This might affect a bankrupt person's ability to buy or rent a home. It might also result in higher interest rates on any loans in the future. Some people who have declared bankruptcy in the past have even had trouble getting utilities such as gas or electricity hooked up in their homes.

"Bankruptcy generally isn't a good idea. Although it probably seems much easier than credit counseling . . . it can haunt you for a good portion of your life," says Tere Stouffer, author of *The Everything Budgeting Book*. "If you have to choose, file Chapter 13. . . . But always meet with a credit-counseling agency before talking to a bankruptcy lawyer. You'll not only save money, you'll preserve your reputation too."[6]

ARE YOU IN TROUBLE WITH DEBT?

Are you confused about whether your financial circumstances are sustainable? Are you worried you've taken on too much bad debt? Answer the following questions to help you get a better idea of your situation.

1. Are your debts making your home, school, or social life unhappy?

2. Do your debts cause you to think less of yourself?

3. Are your debts affecting your reputation with friends or colleagues?

4. Does the pressure of being in debt distract you from your daily work or interrupt your sleeping or eating habits?

5. Have you ever lied about your debt to a parent or guardian, other authority figures, or friends?

6. Have you ever tried to get out of making payments to your creditors or considered bankruptcy?

7. Do you ever worry about whether your employer, family, or friends will find out about the extent of your debt?

8. Has the pressure of your debts ever caused you to use alcohol or drugs or act out?

9. Have you borrowed money without considering whether you can pay back what you owe plus interest?

10. Have you ever created a plan for paying off your debts, only to break it at the last minute?

How did you do? If you answered yes to seven or more of these questions, chances are you have a debt problem. Though it might be stressful, talk to a parent or guardian about what steps you can take to move forward. You could even consult a financial adviser who can help form a plan not only to tackle your debt but also feel better about yourself as you adjust your relationship with money.

SAVING FOR THE FUTURE

Getting out of debt takes dedication and patience. But once debt has either been reduced or eliminated, the work isn't over. Debt management is a continuous process that involves saving and cutting back on spending at the same time.

Think about the following example. Giovanni is 33 years old. In his late teens, he spent his money on things such as a new stereo, a skateboard, and restaurant meals. When he got to college, his spending habits didn't change. Even though he had to pay for books, food, and rent, he still bought a car, went skiing most winter weekends, and ate out instead of cooking. By the time he graduated, he had maxed out three credit cards and was deeply in debt.

Making a budget and sticking to it can help a person get out of debt.

ASK FOR HELP RIGHT AWAY

Davida, who did not give her last name, got a Delta American Express card for the travel benefits. But she didn't pay off the card each month. Instead she just paid the minimum. The interest added up.

"Since then, I've done two balance transfers to 0% APR cards and am working on getting that sucker paid off for good. I keep thinking this will be the year I can get out of debt. Then life happens— unexpected moves, gigs, jobs, surgeries," she said. "I've been lucky to have help from my parents, but I should have summoned the courage to ask [them] for help much sooner."[1]

Giovanni had a difficult time finding a high-paying job after he graduated. Though he worked as a mechanic during the day and played a few gigs as a keyboardist at night, he never had enough money to pay his bills. After the gas company cut off his heat for the second time and he couldn't afford an emergency surgery on his knee after a skiing accident, Giovanni knew he had to take drastic measures. He declared Chapter 13 bankruptcy. After five years, Giovanni paid off his debt and is back to basics. But how can he avoid falling back into debt in the future?

CREATING A BUDGET

Giovanni and others in his situation have several options to prevent debt from resurfacing. Perhaps the most important one is to create a budget. According to the Credit Counseling Society, "since budgeting allows you to create a spending plan for your money, it ensures that you will always have enough money for the things you need and the things that are important to you. Following a budget or spending plan will also keep you out of debt or help you work your way out of debt if you are currently in debt."[2]

The first step to creating a budget is to define any financial goals. Is there any leftover debt that needs to be paid? Are there big purchases on the horizon, such as college

SAMPLE FINANCIAL GOALS

Setting financial goals is especially important for teens because it's a way to prepare for the rest of life. While some goals can be short term, such as saving for a prom dress or a gift, others should be more long term. Examples of realistic long-term financial goals for teens include saving for college, a first apartment, or a volunteer experience in another country. Though saving for retirement might seem too far off the map for some teens, most financial experts agree it's better to be prepared—the earlier the better.

or graduate school, a future home, a car, or some type of medical expense? Start by making a list of all these things.

The next step is to create a spreadsheet of monthly expenses. First, write down all your fixed expenses. These are charges that mostly stay the same every month, such as a phone bill, rent, or cable bill. Next, write down all the variable expenses. These are the charges that vary from month to month, such as money for groceries, movie tickets, or fun activities. Include any payments for long-term planning or retirement, even if the payments aren't made every month. Finally, write down any monthly income and subtract that from the total cost of fixed and variable expenses. That's how much should be spent on clearing out debt or placed in savings.

BUDGET-MAKING APPS

Some people prefer making budgets by hand. Others use computer programs such as Excel to create budgeting spreadsheets. Apps are also available that help people create a budget and keep track of their spending and saving habits in real time. Online reviews of these apps help users find one that makes sense for them.

People can make detailed budgets to stay on track.

Budget

ual Savings	8.415		58.90		10.046
	8.667		72.712		10.349
	8.927		87.738		10.659
	9.195		104.147		10.9
	9.471		122.047		
	9.755		141.554		
	10.048		162.796		
	10.349		185.908		
	10.659		211.034		
	10.979		238.331		
	1.309		267.968		
			300.123		
			7.961		

Additional Income

ount	Details	Month	Amount
4.500	Mid Year Bonus	June	
2.500	Year End Bonus	December	2.000
		January	3.000
			5,000

Planned Expenses

	Expenditure	Month	Amount
	November vacation	November	
	Home for the holidays	December	450
	Gifts for family	December	600
	Family vacation	July	300
		January	880
		January	
Planned Expenses		January	
		January	
			2,230

Annual Budget by Month

arch	April	May	June	July
6,610	9,915	13,220	16,525	21,8
7,000	7,000	7,000	7,000	7.0
0	0	0	7,000	
	3,695	0	2,000	
	0	3,695	3,695	
13,8		0		3,6

"By now, you're probably sick of hearing the 'b' word [budget]. Too bad," says *Investopedia* financial reporter Amy Bell. "This is just one of those financial lessons that cannot be preached enough. Especially in the current turbulent economy, budgeting is more important than ever. If [you] want financial security, following a budget is the *only* answer."[3]

STARTING AN EMERGENCY FUND

A second crucial strategy for avoiding debt is to prepare for it in advance with an emergency fund. An emergency fund is a savings bank account set aside for large, unexpected expenses, such as paying rent after losing a job, covering the cost of a medical issue, or fixing a car after an accident. "One of the first steps in climbing out of debt," says NerdWallet columnist Liz Weston, "is to give yourself a way not to go further into debt."[4] She recommends not touching the account unless there's an actual emergency.

As far as how much to put into the account, financial experts say three to six months' worth of expenses will probably be sufficient for most people. But they also recommend starting small. If you stash a little bit away every two weeks or every month, your emergency account will grow over time. A good way to do that is to create a direct bank transfer from a checking account into the emergency savings account. Even $25 every month helps. "If you don't have any savings, focusing solely on paying debt can backfire when unexpected needs or costs come up," says certified financial planner Melissa Joy. "You might need to borrow again, and debt can become a revolving door."[5]

THE BOTTOM LINE

With all this talk about ways to manage debt, it's tempting to think no one knows how to handle their money. CNBC reported on a 2017 survey that asked 8,000 Americans how much money they've

WHAT'S A HIGH-YIELD SAVINGS ACCOUNT?

When choosing where to store money for an emergency fund, one option is to deposit cash in a bank savings account. Some savings accounts are better than others. Most accumulate around the national average of 0.09 percent interest. But high-interest savings accounts gain as much as 2 percent of compound interest every month.[6] That's money earned on the balance in the account. While 2 percent might not seem like a lot of money, NerdWallet says every little bit helps when trying to both eliminate debt and create an emergency fund. They also suggest high-interest savings accounts as a good option because many have no or low balance requirements to keep the account open.

saved. The survey concluded that 57 percent of Americans don't have $1,000 in their savings accounts. Approximately 39 percent have no savings. What's more, 67 percent of people aged 18 to 24 have less than $1,000 in their savings account, while 46 percent have none at all.[7]

But a 2017 survey by financial group TD Ameritrade suggests teens are actually off to a promising start when it comes to budgeting and controlling their finances. They've also developed some fairly responsible moneymaking habits. According to the survey, approximately 40 percent of teens create and try to follow a budget. About one-half of them have jobs outside their homes. On average, they earn $465 a month. More than 50 percent of teens who are earning money put at least some of that money into savings. Approximately 33 percent are managing to save an average of at least $290 a month—that's a total of $14,000 after four years of high school.[8]

Managing debt is something everyone has to deal with at every stage of life after early adolescence. But though there's always more to learn, today's teens seem to be on the right track. "Though you'd think the opposite would be true, today's teenagers seem to know a lot about saving money and planning

Unexpected hospital visits can be expensive.

SAMPLE WAYS TO REDUCE DEBT

In addition to creating a budget and setting up an emergency fund, people do other things to reduce debt while saving for the future. One option is to keep a coin jar. While it may not seem like much at first, throwing loose change into a can or glass jug can add up quickly. Make sure the container is sealed and can't be opened until the jar is full. That way, there won't be a temptation to spend the money. In addition, create a debt-takedown challenge. Make a pact with a friend to either get rid of debt or start a savings plan. Set milestones, see who accomplishes each goal first, and stage small celebrations when goals are met.

responsibly for the future," says personal finance reporter Maurie Backman. She also has a word of advice for adults: "If you're among the countless adults who have yet to prioritize short-term or retirement savings, you may want to pay attention to what the young adults in your life are doing with their finances. They just might teach you a thing or two."[9]

Teens can save money to achieve their financial goals.

CREATING A BUDGET: MONTHLY EXPENSES

Use this form to create a monthly budget. Fill it out each month to see how your spending habits change and where you might improve to save money and pay down debt.

Item	$ Amount Budgeted	$ Amount Spent
Food		
Groceries		
Snacks/Coffee		
Dining Out		
TOTAL:		
Transportation		
Car Payments		
Gas/Fuel		
Repairs/Maintenance		
Public Transportation		
TOTAL:		
Entertainment		
Movies/Concerts		
Books/Music		
Sports		
Other Hobbies		
TOTAL:		

Item	$ Amount Budgeted	$ Amount Spent
Personal		
Clothing/Shoes		
Personal Grooming		
Gym Membership		
Gifts		
Miscellaneous		
TOTAL:		
Utilities (If Applicable)		
Cable TV/Internet		
Cell Phone		
Gas		
Electric		
Other		
TOTAL:		
Debt Payments		
Credit/Debit Cards		
Student Loans		
Other Loans		
Savings Payments		
College		
Emergency Fund		
Retirement		
TOTAL:		
$ GRAND TOTAL		

KEY TAKEAWAYS

TOP 10 MOST IMPORTANT CONCEPTS

1. Debt can happen to anyone if they aren't careful with how they spend money.

2. There are two types of debt. Good debt helps borrowers build credit and create a brighter future. Examples of good debt are student loans and mortgages.

3. Bad debt is the type of debt that is best avoided whenever possible. Examples of bad debt are insurmountable credit card bills and payday loans.

4. People younger than 21 have two options for credit cards: secured credit cards or becoming an authorized user on a parent or guardian's account. Paying off the bill each month is essential to staying out of debt.

5. A credit score is similar to a report card showing how a person handles his or her money.

6. People with above-average FICO scores qualify for lower interest rates, car insurance rates, and mortgage rates. People with bad scores are seen as risky by lenders.

7. Paying off a large amount of debt can be done two ways. Debt laddering means tackling high-interest credit cards and loans first. Debt snowballing is paying off bills with the lowest balance first. This may accrue more interest

over time, but it can provide the debtor with a sense of accomplishment.

8. Chapter 7 and Chapter 13 are two major types of bankruptcy. Both should be viewed as a last resort when managing debt.

9. Bankruptcy stays on a person's record for ten years. It can affect future employment, the ability to buy a home, and sometimes even getting utility services installed.

10. A smart way to avoid bad debt in the future is to set up an emergency fund.

TOP 5 TAKEAWAYS

1. Never max out credit cards, and always pay off balances in full and on time every month.

2. Set up automatic payments to ensure bills are paid on time.

3. Create a budget to keep spending under control. Stick to your budget, no matter what.

4. In addition to being proactive about saving for the future, set money aside for emergencies.

5. If you're having trouble managing or paying off debt, ask a parent or guardian for help or consult a financial adviser.

GLOSSARY

alimony
Money a person is legally bound to pay to his or her spouse following a divorce.

annual percentage rate (APR)
Interest, calculated annually, that is charged on a loan or earned on an investment.

bankruptcy
A legal proceeding where a person tells a judge that he or she can't pay his or her debts.

cosigner
A person who agrees to take on a joint obligation to pay back a debt, such as a parent who cosigns on a car loan for his or her child.

credit bureau
Businesses that record credit activity for consumers and report this information in the form of credit reports.

credit score
A number assigned to an individual that predicts his or her ability to repay a loan.

down payment
Money paid up front when purchasing something on credit; the payment is usually a percentage of the total cost of the item.

economist

A person who studies society's choices about the way goods and services are produced, distributed, and consumed, as well as the consequences of those choices.

freelancer

A person who works for different companies at different times rather than being permanently employed by one company.

frugal

Responsible and careful when spending money; not spending a lot of money.

interest

A fee charged when a person or business borrows money, or money paid to people as an incentive for keeping their money in a bank.

mortgage

A legal agreement by which a bank or other creditor lends money at interest in exchange for taking title of the debtor's property.

revenue

Income, especially of a company or organization and of a substantial nature.

ADDITIONAL RESOURCES

SELECTED BIBLIOGRAPHY

El Issa, Erin. "NerdWallet's 2017 American Household Credit Card Debt Study," *NerdWallet*, n.d., nerdwallet.com. Accessed 13 Nov. 2018.

Romans, Christine. *Smart Is the New Rich: Money Guide for Millennials.* Wiley, 2015.

Stouffer, Tere. *The Everything Budgeting Book.* Adams Media, 2013.

FURTHER READINGS

Edwards, Sue Bradford. *Earning, Saving, and Investing.* Abdo, 2020.

Regan, Michael. *The Cost of College.* Abdo, 2020.

ONLINE RESOURCES

Booklinks
NONFICTION NETWORK
FREE! ONLINE NONFICTION RESOURCES

To learn more about managing debt, please visit **abdobooklinks.com** or scan this QR code. These links are routinely monitored and updated to provide the most current information available.

MORE INFORMATION

For more information on this subject, contact or visit the following organizations:

BRAIN ARTS PRODUCTIONS
3502 N. Elston Ave.
Chicago, IL 60647
773-850-2199
brainartsproductions.org
This organization offers programs on how to create a business, understand economic theories, and pay off debt.

FEDERAL RESERVE BANK OF NEW YORK
33 Liberty St.
New York, NY 10045
212-720-5000
newyorkfed.org
The Federal Reserve Bank of New York offers tours, workshops, and seminars about finances and economics to students at all education levels.

SOURCE NOTES

CHAPTER 1. SWIMMING IN DEBT

1. Hayley Peterson. "Teens Have a New Favorite Restaurant—and It's Not Starbucks." *Business Insider*, 11 Apr. 2017, businessinsider.com. Accessed 25 Jan. 2019.
2. Paul Golden. "American Students Struggle to Demonstrate Financial Capability on International Stage." *National Endowment for Financial Education*, 24 May 2017, nefe.org. Accessed 25 Jan. 2019.
3. Sophia Rase. "Three Money Conversations Every Teen Should Have with Their Parents." *Money*, 8 Nov. 2017, money.com. Accessed 25 Jan. 2019.

CHAPTER 2. SLOPPY SPENDING

1. Kerri Anne Renzulli. "This Is How Much Debt the Average American Has Now—at Every Age." *Money*, 13 Apr. 2018, money.com. Accessed 25 Jan. 2019.
2. Renzulli, "This Is How Much Debt the Average American Has Now."
3. Maurie Backman. "It's Official: Most Americans Are Currently in Debt." *Motley Fool*, 15 Feb. 2018, fool.com. Accessed 25 Jan. 2019.
4. "The Details of Debt." *Comet*, n.d., cometfi.com. Accessed 25 Jan. 2019.
5. Tim Lemke. "8 Common Causes of Debt—and How to Avoid Them." *Wise Bread*, 15 Feb. 2018, wisebread.com. Accessed 25 Jan. 2019.
6. Courtney Jespersen. "Needs vs. Wants: How to Distinguish and Budget for Both." *NerdWallet*, 8 Mar. 2017, nerdwallet.com. Accessed 25 Jan. 2019.
7. Jespersen, "Needs vs. Wants."
8. Lemke, "8 Common Causes of Debt."
9. "Overshopping/Overspending." *Shulman Center*, n.d., theshulmancenter.com. Accessed 25 Jan. 2019.

CHAPTER 3. GOOD DEBT

1. Dave Roos. "How Debt Works." *How Stuff Works*, n.d., money.howstuffworks.com. Accessed 25 Jan. 2019.
2. Roos, "How Debt Works."
3. Abigail Hess. "Here's How Much the Average Student Loan Borrower Owes When They Graduate." *CNBC*, 15 Feb. 2018, cnbc.com. Accessed 25 Jan. 2019.
4. Hess, "Here's How Much the Average Student Loan Borrower Owes When They Graduate."
5. "Trends in Higher Education." *College Board*, n.d., trends.collegeboard.org. Accessed 25 Jan. 2019.
6. Hess, "Here's How Much the Average Student Loan Borrower Owes When They Graduate."
7. Niall McCarthy. "How US Education Has Become 'A Debt Sentence' [Infographic]." *Forbes*, 27 Aug. 2018, forbes.com. Accessed 25 Jan. 2019.

8. Hess, "Here's How Much the Average Student Loan Borrower Owes When They Graduate."
9. "Mortgage Debt Outstanding." *Federal Reserve*, n.d., federalreserve.gov. Accessed 25 Jan. 2019.
10. Roos, "How Debt Works."
11. Damian Davila. "10 Smart Ways to Get a Small Business Loan." *Wise Bread*, 12 July 2018, wisebread.com. Accessed 25 Jan. 2019.

CHAPTER 4. BAD DEBT

1. Dave Roos. "How Debt Works." *How Stuff Works*, n.d., money.howstuffworks.com. Accessed 25 Jan. 2019.
2. Megan Elliott. "11 Dirty Secrets You Don't Know about Pawn Shops." *Cheat Sheet*, 3 Apr. 2018, cheatsheet.com. Accessed 25 Jan. 2019.
3. "Payday Loan Facts and the CFPB's Impact." *Pew Charitable Trust*, 14 Jan. 2016, pewtrusts.org. Accessed 25 Jan. 2019.
4. Kevin Mercadante. "What Is a Payday Loan and Why Is It A REALLY Bad Idea to Get One?" *Money Under 30*, 26 Oct. 2017, moneyunder30.com. Accessed 25 Jan. 2019.
5. Mercadante, "What Is a Payday Loan and Why Is It A REALLY Bad Idea to Get One?"
6. Claire Tsosie and Erin El Issa. "2018 American Household Credit Card Debt Study." *NerdWallet*, 10 Dec. 2018, nerdwallet.com. Accessed 25 Jan. 2019.
7. Melissa Lambarena. "Save Big with These Pre-Holiday Credit Card Strategies." *NerdWallet*, 10 Oct. 2018, nerdwallet.com. Accessed 25 Jan. 2019.
8. Erin El Issa. "2017 American Household Credit Card Debt Study." *NerdWallet*, n.d., nerdwallet.com. Accessed 25 Jan. 2019.
9. Jessica Dickler. "Why Credit Card Debt Can Be Bad for Your Health." *CNBC*, 13 Feb. 2019, cnbc.com. Accessed 25 Jan. 2019.

CHAPTER 5. THE LOWDOWN ON CREDIT CARDS

1. "Credit Card Facts." *Mint*, n.d., themint.org. Accessed 25 Jan. 2019.
2. "Credit Card Facts."
3. Melanie Lockert. "9 Different Credit Card Types to Consider." *Credit Karma*, 23 Jan. 2019, creditkarma.com. Accessed 25 Jan. 2019.
4. "NerdWallet's Best Premium Credit Cards of 2018." *NerdWallet*, n.d., nerdwallet.com. Accessed 5 Nov. 2018.
5. John Kiernan. "What Are the Best Credit Cards for Teens?" *Wallet Hub*, 25 July 2018, wallethub.com. Accessed 5 Nov. 2018.
6. Lockert, "9 Different Credit Card Types to Consider."
7. Christine Romans. *Smart Is the New Rich: Money Guide for Millennials.* Wiley, 2015. 131.

CHAPTER 6. BUILDING GOOD CREDIT

1. "What Is a Good Credit Score?" *Experian*, n.d., experian.com. Accessed 25 Jan. 2019.

SOURCE NOTES CONTINUED

2. Christine Romans. *Smart Is the New Rich: Money Guide for Millennials*. Wiley, 2015. 134.
3. Leslie McFadden. "8 Major Benefits of New Credit Card Law." *Bankrate*, 20 Aug. 2018, bankrate.com. Accessed 25 Jan. 2019.
4. McFadden, "8 Major Benefits of New Credit Card Law."
5. Romans, *Smart Is the New Rich*, 132.
6. Romans, *Smart Is the New Rich*, 132.
7. "Not-So-Obvious Causes for a Dropping FICO Score." *My FICO*, n.d., myfico.com. Accessed 25 Jan. 2019.

CHAPTER 7. PAYING DOWN DEBT
1. Tamsen Butler. *The Complete Guide to Personal Finance*. Atlantic, 2016. 182.
2. Butler, *The Complete Guide to Personal Finance*, 183–184.
3. Dave Roos. "How Debt Works." *How Stuff Works*, n.d., money.howstuffworks.com. Accessed 25 Jan. 2019.
4. Sean Pyles. "How Much Bankruptcy Costs and How to Pay for It." *NerdWallet*, 12 Mar. 2018, nerdwallet.com. Accessed 25 Jan. 2019.
5. Tere Stouffer. *The Everything Budgeting Book*. Adams Media, 2013. 182–183.
6. Stouffer, *The Everything Budgeting Book*, 179.

CHAPTER 8. SAVING FOR THE FUTURE
1. "5 Cautionary Credit Card Tales." *Beth Kobliner*, 23 Aug. 2017, bethkobliner.com. Accessed 25 Jan. 2019.
2. "What Is Budgeting? What Is a Budget?" *My Money Coach*, n.d., mymoneycoach.ca. Accessed 25 Jan. 2019.
3. Amy Bell. "6 Reasons Why You NEED a Budget." *Investopedia*, 29 Sept. 2017, investopedia.com. Accessed 25 Jan. 2019.
4. Spencer Tierney. "Emergency Fund: What It Is and Why It Matters." *NerdWallet*, 30 Nov. 2017, nerdwallet.com. Accessed 25 Jan. 2019.
5. Amy Fontinelle. "Should You Pay Debts First or Save? Use These Guidelines to Decide." *Bankrate*, 1 Oct. 2018, bankrate.com. Accessed 25 Jan. 2019.
6. Spencer Tierney. "Best High-Yield Online Savings Accounts of 2018." *NerdWallet*, n.d., nerdwallet.com. Accessed 5 Nov. 2018.
7. Kathleen Elkins. "Here's How Much Money the Average Millennial Has in Savings." *CNBC*, 14 Sept. 2017, cnbc.com. Accessed 25 Jan. 2019.
8. Maurie Backman. "7 Stats That Show How Today's Teens Are Making Smart Money Choices." *Motley Fool*, 23 July 2017, fool.com. Accessed 25 Jan. 2019.
9. Backman, "7 Stats That Show How Today's Teens Are Making Smart Money Choices."

INDEX

INDEX CONTINUED

ABOUT THE AUTHOR

Alexis Burling has written dozens of articles and books for young readers on a variety of topics, including current events, biographies of famous people, nutrition, fitness, careers, and money management. She is also a professional book critic with reviews of adult and young adult books, author interviews, and other publishing industry–related articles featured in the *New York Times*, the *Washington Post*, *San Francisco Chronicle*, and more. She lives in Portland, Oregon, with her husband.

ABOUT THE CONSULTANT

Robert Kelchen is an assistant professor of higher education at Seton Hall University in New Jersey. His research focuses on college affordability and student loan debt, and he has been quoted in the *New York Times*, the *Wall Street Journal*, the *Washington Post*, and more. He and his wife are nearly finished paying off her law school debt, which was a great investment but required careful budgeting to pay off within ten years.